ONE DAY

BY THE NUMBERS

STEVE JENKINS

CLARION BOOKS
AN IMPRINT OF HARPERCOLLINSPUBLISHERS
Boston   New York

Contents

5   Introduction

6   How much do animals eat?

8   The animals we eat

10   Deadly animals

12   Divide and conquer

14   Just discovered

15   Gone forever

16   Migrating animals

18   Human-powered

20   Along for the ride

22   A 24-hour body

24   New life — and death

26   Daily disasters

28   A day of flames

29   Melting ice

30   Fresh water

32   Forests lost . . .

33   . . . and deserts gained

34   Daily energy use

36   The modern world

38/39   Glossary & Bibliography

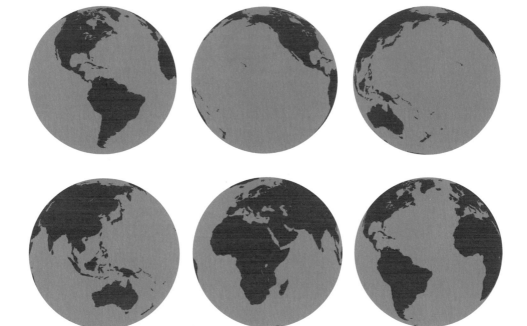

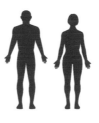

You might be surprised at what happens in just one day. Did you know that we travel more than one and a half million miles as the earth orbits the sun? Or that almost 400,000 babies are born? Or that a hummingbird can fly 500 miles without taking a break?

A lot goes on in 24 hours, from the 100,000 beats of your heart to the dozens of deadly natural disasters that take place around the world.

The infographics in this book — charts, graphs, diagrams, and illustrations — can help us understand some of these fascinating daily events.

How much do animals eat in one day?

Big animals eat a lot. Some of them eat tons of food every day. But compared to their body weight, small animals consume more food than big ones.

Each full circle represents an animal's body weight. The red section shows the weight of the food it eats every day.

A **shrew** must eat its body weight in food each day. If the shrew goes more than a few hours without eating, it will starve to death.

A **hummingbird**'s wings beat so quickly that they look like a blur to us. This takes a lot of energy — a lot of food.

A **panda** may spend 16 hours a day eating. In that time, it can devour 40 pounds (18 kilograms) of bamboo.

An **adult blue whale** consumes four tons, or 8,000 pounds (3,630 kilograms), of krill* each day.

As it feeds on its mother's rich milk, a **baby blue whale** can gain 250 pounds (113 kilograms) every 24 hours.

Elephants eat grass and leaves. These foods aren't very nutritious, so an elephant must eat a lot of them — 200 to 400 pounds (90 to 180 kilograms) daily.

* *Words in blue can be found in the glossary on page 38.*

The animals we eat

Every day, people around the world eat billions of animals. Each silhouette on this page represents one million animals.

sheep
1½ million

goats
1⅕ million

geese
2 million

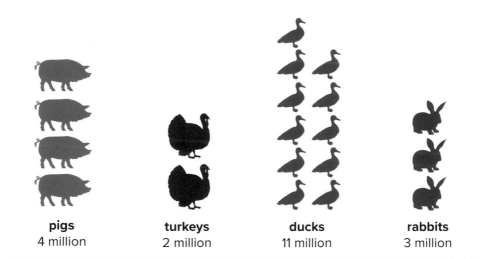

pigs
4 million

turkeys
2 million

ducks
11 million

rabbits
3 million

cows
800,000

We eat so many chickens and fish that a different scale is needed for these creatures. Each silhouette on this page represents one hundred million animals eaten daily.

chickens
180 million

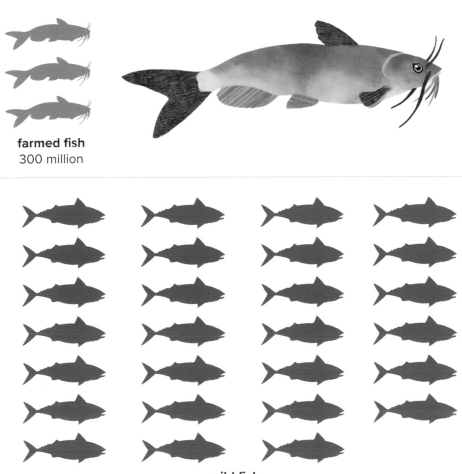

farmed fish
300 million

wild fish
2,700 million

How many humans are killed by animals in a day?

People kill billions of animals every day, mostly for food. But there are some animals that kill people. Sometimes they kill humans for food. But most human deaths happen when creatures defend themselves or transmit deadly diseases.

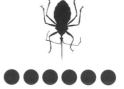

crocodile
3 people

tsetse fly
25 people

roundworm
5 people

assassin bug
30 people

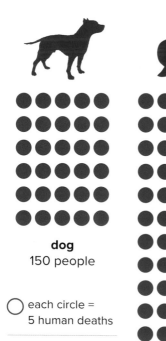

dog
150 people

○ each circle =
5 human deaths

● physical injury

● disease

● venom

freshwater snail
275 people

snake
275 people

Sharks are one of the most feared animals on earth, but they kill only about one person every month or two.

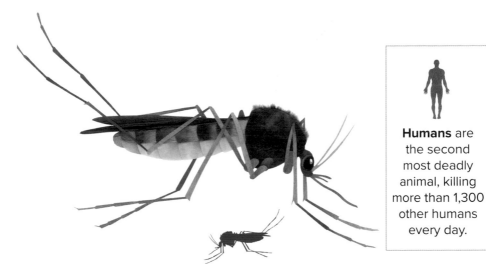

Humans are the second most deadly animal, killing more than 1,300 other humans every day.

mosquito
2,500 people

Divide and conquer

Yeast is a common microscopic organism. Some varieties are used by bakers to help make bread rise.

A yeast cell reproduces by budding, creating a duplicate cell every 100 minutes. One yeast cell can produce more than 8,000 offspring in 24 hours.

Just discovered

Millions of organisms are still unknown to science. The plants and animals shown here weren't found on the same day. But an average of 50 new species are named each day.

A new kind of **leaf-tailed gecko** found in Australia

A previously unknown species of **pitcher plant** that grows in Cambodia

A **cave-dwelling beetle** from China

The **olinguito**, a South American mammal

new species discovered in one day		
species that go extinct in one day		
number of species	50	100

Gone forever

These plants and animal didn't become extinct at the same time. But an estimated 150–200 species vanish every 24 hours.

The **Spix's macaw** was native to Brazil. (Extinct in the wild in 2000)

This **maidenhair fern** grew in China. (Extinct in 2004)

The **scimitar-horned oryx** lived in North Africa. (Probably extinct in the wild in 1980)

When he died, Lonely George was the last **Hawaiian tree snail** of his kind. (Extinct in 2019)

The **West African black rhinoceros** was once found throughout Central Africa. (Extinct in 2003)

The **golden toad** lived in the mountains of Costa Rica. (Extinct in 2004)

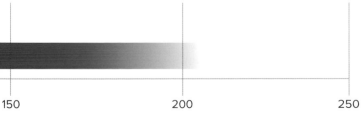

150   200   250

How far do migrating animals travel in a day?

Many animals migrate. They often travel great distances — sometimes thousands of miles — to find food, a mate, or a more favorable climate. How far can these creatures go in 24 hours as they migrate?

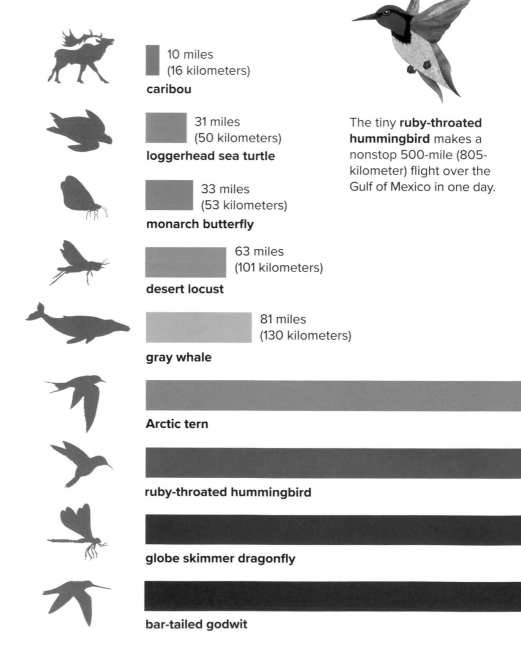

10 miles
(16 kilometers)
caribou

31 miles
(50 kilometers)
loggerhead sea turtle

33 miles
(53 kilometers)
monarch butterfly

63 miles
(101 kilometers)
desert locust

81 miles
(130 kilometers)
gray whale

Arctic tern

ruby-throated hummingbird

globe skimmer dragonfly

bar-tailed godwit

The tiny **ruby-throated hummingbird** makes a nonstop 500-mile (805-kilometer) flight over the Gulf of Mexico in one day.

The 24-hour animal distance champion may be the **bar-tailed godwit**. It makes a nonstop 7,000-mile (11,265-kilometer) flight from Alaska to New Zealand every fall. As it migrates, this little bird covers 750 miles or more every 24 hours.

During its six-month migration, the **gray whale** may travel 14,000 miles (22,531 kilometers). It can swim more than 80 miles a day.

400 miles (644 kilometers)

500 miles (805 kilometers)

528 miles (850 kilometers)

750 miles (1,207 kilometers)

How far can we travel in a day under our own power?

These are 24-hour distance records for human-powered travel.

**64 miles
(103 kilometers)**

swimming

**142 miles
(229 kilometers)**

walking

**281 miles
(452 kilometers)**

riding a unicycle

**293 miles
(472 kilometers)**

Nordic skiing

 The full circle represents a distance of 700 miles (1,127 kilometers).

152 miles
(245 kilometers)

188½ miles
(303 kilometers)

paddling a kayak

running

338 miles
(544 kilometers)

569 miles
(916 kilometers)

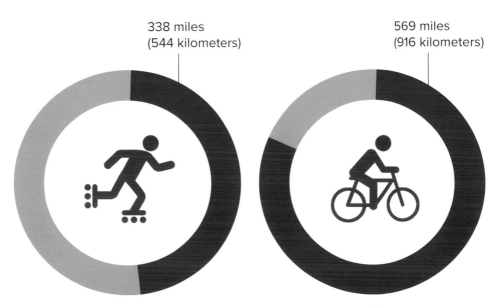

in-line skating

cycling

How far do we travel in 24 hours as we go along for the ride?

The earth is spinning and moving through space, and we move with it.

A person standing on the equator travels 25,000 miles (40,233 kilometers) around the center of the earth as the planet rotates.

The earth is spinning, but we don't feel its motion. Instead, it looks to us like the sun, moon, and stars are moving across the sky.

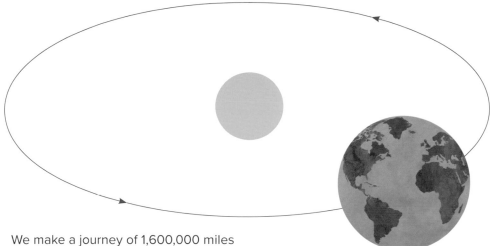

We make a journey of 1,600,000 miles (2,575,000 kilometers) every 24 hours as the earth orbits the sun. This is farther than three trips to the moon and back.

Our solar system circles the center of the Milky Way galaxy. Every 24 hours, our sun and its planets travel more than 12 million miles (19 million kilometers) on this journey. Even so, it will take 230 million years to make a complete trip around the galaxy.

We are here.

A 24-hour body

Every day, our bodies constantly pump blood, breathe air, shed millions of cells, and do many other things that we rarely notice.

Most people lose 50 to 100 hairs from their head each day.

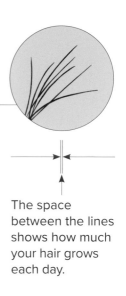

The space between the lines shows how much your hair grows each day.

Humans blink about 17,000 times a day.

Each of us produces up to 48 ounces (1½ liters) of urine, or pee, a day.

Humans eat an average of four pounds (1,814 grams) of food a day.

An adult human heart beats about 100,000 times a day, and pumps enough blood to fill 32 55-gallon (208-liter) barrels.

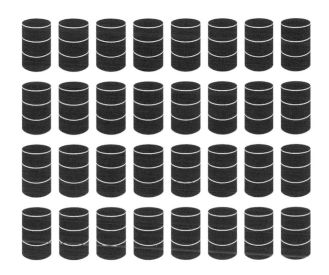

A 55-gallon barrel compared to an adult woman

We shed about 500 million skin cells every day.

An average person takes 20,000 breaths each day. They move enough air in and out of their lungs to fill a balloon more than nine feet ($2^3/_4$ meters) in diameter.

New life — and death

How many people are born each day?
And how many people die?

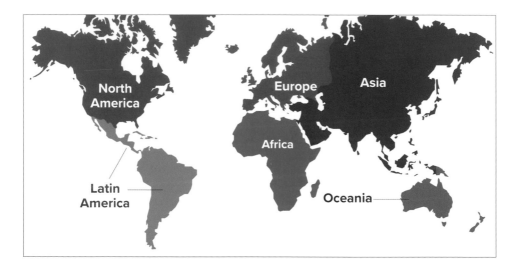

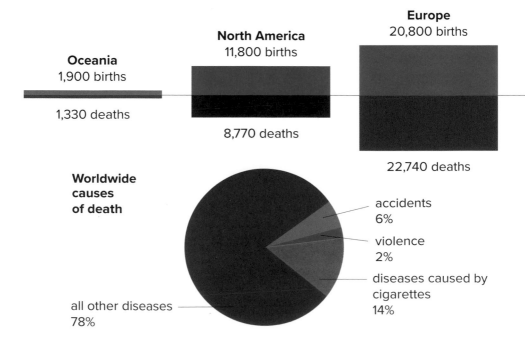

Oceania
1,900 births

1,330 deaths

North America
11,800 births

8,770 deaths

Europe
20,800 births

22,740 deaths

**Worldwide
causes
of death**

accidents
6%

violence
2%

diseases caused by
cigarettes
14%

all other diseases
78%

In Europe, where the median age is 43, there are more deaths than births. In Africa, however, the median age is less than 20. On that continent, there are many more births than deaths.

Asia
202,190 births

Africa
118,360 births

Latin America
28,770 births

11,340 deaths

29,490 deaths

Around the world, approximately 384,000 babies are born every day and 161,000 people die (2020 totals).

87,670 deaths

Daily disasters

Earthquakes, tornadoes, and other dramatic natural events are unpredictable. But they happen somewhere on earth every day.

small earthquakes
(magnitude 2.5 or less)

How many earthquakes occur each day?

moderate earthquakes
(magnitude 5.4 to 6.0)

minor earthquakes
(magnitude 2.5 to 5.4)

4 a day

80 a day

2,500 a day

In these earthquakes, shaking is quite noticeable. There can be slight damage to buildings.

These quakes are not as strong, but are usually noticeable. Objects may fall off shelves.

These small quakes are detected by scientific instruments. They are not usually felt by people.

How many tornadoes occur daily?

On average, there are four tornadoes a day somewhere in the world. Eighty percent of all tornadoes form in the United States and Canada.

Lightning strikes

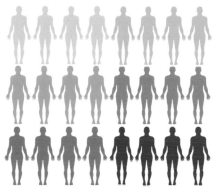

Lightning strikes somewhere on earth almost four million times a day.

Between four and twenty-four people are killed by lightning every day.

How many volcanic eruptions take place in a day?

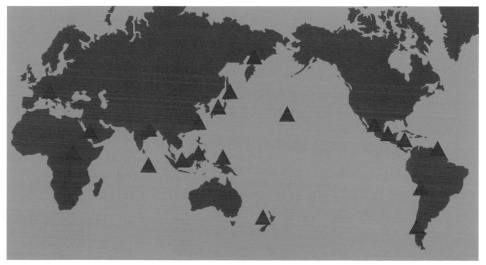

Worldwide, an average of 20 volcanoes erupt each day.

A day of flames

Thousands of wildfires are burning somewhere around the world each day.

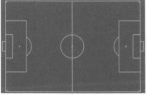

Every day, an area of forest or grassland equal in size to 125,000 soccer fields is burned by wildfires.

Wildfires are growing more frequent and more intense as the climate gets hotter. Humans have caused much of the increase in the earth's temperature by burning coal, oil, and gas.

What causes wildfires?
Note: Wildfire causes vary from place to place — these are averages.

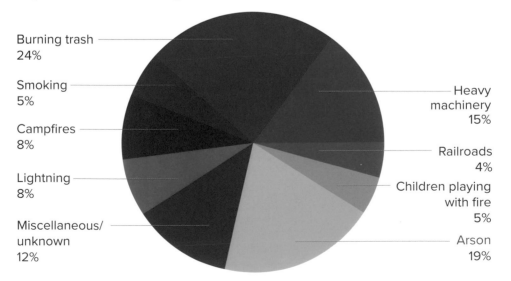

Burning trash
24%

Smoking
5%

Campfires
8%

Lightning
8%

Miscellaneous/
unknown
12%

Heavy
machinery
15%

Railroads
4%

Children playing
with fire
5%

Arson
19%

How much ice melts in a day?

Two-thirds of the world's fresh water is frozen in ice sheets and glaciers. This snow and ice is melting at an increasing rate as the world heats up.

Antarctica

Ice sheets are thick layers of ice that rest on land. The Antarctic ice sheet holds 90 percent of the earth's ice and snow. Most of the rest is in the Greenland ice sheet.

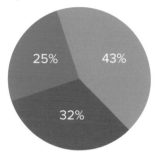

A glacier is a slowly moving mass of ice formed by the accumulation of snow over many years. Glaciers are found in the mountains of every continent except Australia.

Where is the ice melting?

- mountain glaciers
- Greenland ice sheet
- Antarctic ice sheet

The earth's glaciers are melting more quickly than in the past. They hold only about 1 percent of the world's ice, but they are responsible for much of the ice loss.

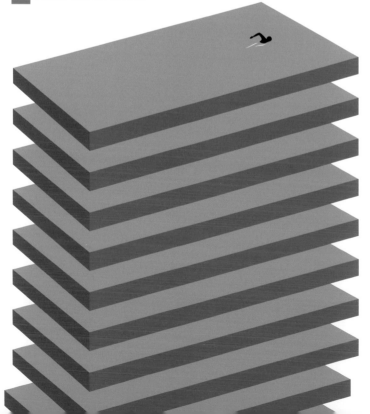

Every day, on average, enough of the earth's ice melts to fill more than 16,000 Olympic-size swimming pools.

Fresh water

Almost all of the earth's liquid water is in the oceans. And much of the water that isn't salty seawater is frozen or locked deep underground.

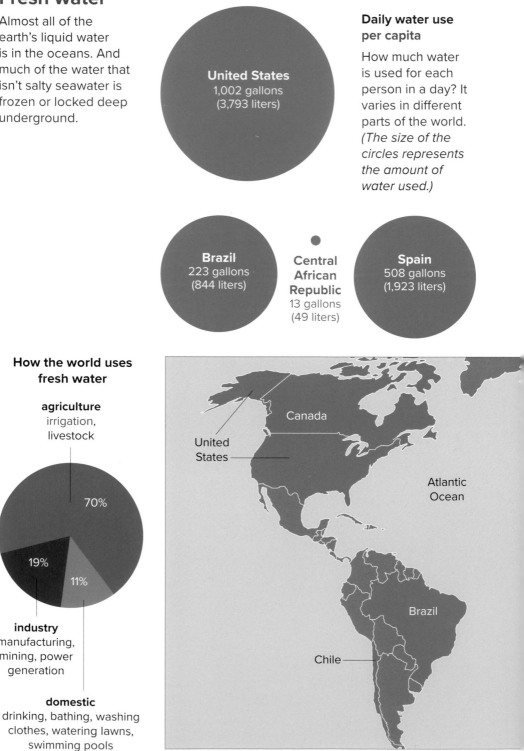

United States
1,002 gallons
(3,793 liters)

Daily water use per capita

How much water is used for each person in a day? It varies in different parts of the world. *(The size of the circles represents the amount of water used.)*

Brazil
223 gallons
(844 liters)

Central African Republic
13 gallons
(49 liters)

Spain
508 gallons
(1,923 liters)

How the world uses fresh water

agriculture
irrigation, livestock

70%

19%

11%

industry
manufacturing, mining, power generation

domestic
drinking, bathing, washing clothes, watering lawns, swimming pools

Canada

United States

Atlantic Ocean

Brazil

Chile

Canada
718 gallons
(2,718 liters)

Chile
1,568 gallons
(5,936 liters)

Denmark
84 gallons
(318 liters)

India
446 gallons
(1,668 liters)

China
308 gallons
(1,166 liters)

Russia
346 gallons
(1,310 liters)

Australia
481 gallons
(1,821 liters)

Denmark

Russia

Spain

China

Pacific
Ocean

India

Central
African
Republic

Indian
Ocean

Australia

Forests lost . . .

Forests cover almost one-third of the earth's land, but they are being lost at a rapid rate. An area of forest equal in size to about 40,000 soccer fields is cut down or intentionally burned every day.

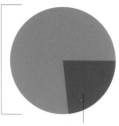

forest cut down or burned daily

rainforest

Causes of deforestation

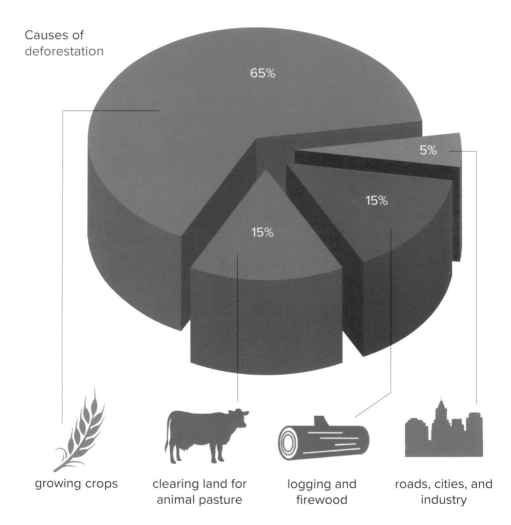

65%

15%

15%

5%

growing crops

clearing land for animal pasture

logging and firewood

roads, cities, and industry

Around the world, an estimated 41 million trees are cut down every day.

. . . and deserts gained

Over-farming, drought, and climate change are turning grassland, farmland, and pasture into desert.

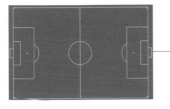

This tiny green rectangle shows the size of a soccer field compared to the amount of land that is turning into desert around the world every day.

Daily energy use

Most of the energy we use comes from fossil fuels, including coal, oil, and natural gas. Burning fossil fuels — especially coal — releases gases that are causing our climate to heat up. These fuels are gradually being replaced by cleaner forms of energy such as hydroelectric, wind, and solar power.

This building is more than 100 feet (30 meters) tall.

The amount of coal burned around the world every day compared to a 10-story building.

Almost all of our energy comes from the sun.*

Wind is created by the sun heating the atmosphere. Fossil fuels release energy from sunlight that was captured and stored by plants millions of years ago. Even hydroelectric power, which is produced by water, relies on the power of the sun to create precipitation.

The coal burned daily could fill 200,000 train cars.

* The exceptions are nuclear energy, which relies on the decay of radioactive elements, and thermal energy, which comes from volcanic sources inside the earth..

Around the world, people use about 95 million barrels, or four billion gallons (15 billion liters), of oil every day. This is about one-half gallon of oil per person each day.

Some countries use more oil than others.

Gallons (liters) of oil used daily per person

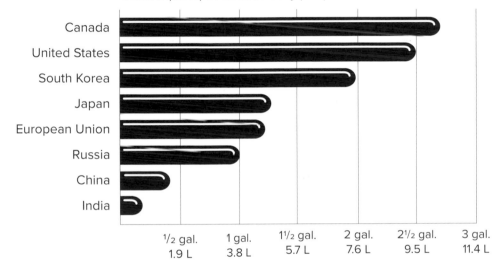

Canada					
United States					
South Korea					
Japan					
European Union					
Russia					
China					
India					

½ gal.	1 gal.	1½ gal.	2 gal.	2½ gal.	3 gal.
1.9 L	3.8 L	5.7 L	7.6 L	9.5 L	11.4 L

The world's energy sources

When all sources of energy are combined, the world uses the energy equivalent of 280 million barrels of oil a day.

oil
33%

natural gas
24%

wind, solar, biomass
5%

hydroelectric (water)
6%

nuclear
5%

coal
27%

The modern world

Here are some surprising facts and figures about things we make, consume, and throw away — every day.

Around the world, 266,000 new cars are built.

Six thousand new books are published.

More than 15 billion cigarettes are smoked (and 27,000 people die from smoking).

More than 580,000 new televisions are manufactured.

Almost four billion 12-ounce soft drinks are consumed.

Around 175,000 commercial flights take off (not including personal aircraft or military flights).

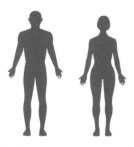

And about 12 million people fly somewhere.

Each day, 50 million pounds of plastic waste make their way into the ocean. That's the equivalent of more than two billion plastic water bottles.

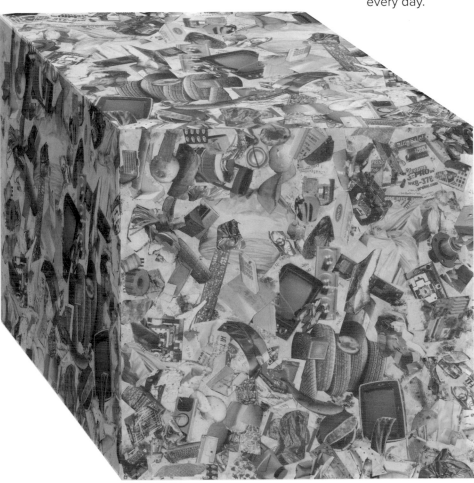

The world's daily trash production (below) compared to a 10-story building

More than four million cell phones are sold every day.

Glossary

arson
The criminal act of starting a fire that burns a building, forest, or other property.

biomass
The total weight of the plants and/or animals in a specific area.

budding

A kind of reproduction in which a new organism is formed by an outgrowth of cells — a bud — on a preexisting organism.

deforestation
Cutting down or burning trees over a large area.

drought
A long period of time with less rain or snowfall than normal.

energy equivalent
A way to measure the amount of energy in one fuel source by comparing it to the amount of energy in another fuel source.

equator
An imaginary line halfway between the North and South Poles that divides the earth into equal hemispheres.

extinct
No longer living. The term is applied to a particular species or group of organisms, not an individual.

fossil fuels
Gas, coal, and oil — fuels created by the remains of plants and animals that lived millions of years ago.

hydroelectric power
Electricity generated by falling or flowing water.

ice sheet
A layer of ice that covers a large area, but not as large as an ice cap. It can be on land or floating on water.

irrigation
Pumping and/or spraying water to help crops grow rather than depending on natural precipitation.

krill
Small, shrimp-like animals that live in the sea. They gather by the billions in swarms that provide food for many larger animals.

median
The midpoint in an ordered series of numbers.

Milky Way galaxy
A galaxy is a large group of stars bound together by gravity. Our sun is one of the 100 billion to 400 billion stars in the Milky Way galaxy, an enormous flat disk with spiral arms.

Nordic skiing
Cross-country skiing. Named after the Nordic — or Scandinavian — countries where the sport originated.

nuclear energy
Energy produced by splitting uranium atoms in a process called fission. Heat from this reaction is used to generate electricity.

nutritious
Food that provides nourishment; healthy food and diet.

organisms
Any living thing, including plants, animals, and single-cell life forms.

per capita
Per person.

precipitation
Rain, snow, hail, or sleet; water in any form that falls to the ground as part of a natural process.

radioactive elements
Matter composed of unstable atoms that emit particles and release energy.

rise
In the context of baking, yeast produces gas that forms tiny bubbles and causes bread dough to rise.

scientific instruments
Tools used to observe and measure natural or human-made events or processes.

solar power
Power generated by converting the sun's rays into electricity.

Bibliography

Animal Records.
By Mark Carwardine. Sterling, 2008.

Big Numbers. By Mary & John Gribbin. Wizard Books, 2003.

The Book of Comparisons. By Clive Gifford. Ivy Kids, 2018.

The Earth Book. By Jonathon Litton. 360 Degrees, 2017.

Earth-Shattering Events. By Robin Jacobs. Cicada Books, 2019.

Global Warming. By Seymour Simon. Harper Collins, 2013.

Information Everywhere. Edited by Jenny Finch. DK Publishing, 2013.

Life. By Martha Holmes and Michael Gunton. BBC Books, 2009.

Sciencia. By Burkard Polster, Matthew Watkins, Matt Tweed, Gerard Cheshire, and Moff Betts. Wooden Books, 2011.

The Sizesaurus. By Stephen Strauss. Kodansha International, 1995.

Supernavigators. By David Barrie. The Experiment, 2019.

For Jeffrey

Clarion Books is an imprint of HarperCollins Publishers.

One Day by the Numbers
Copyright © 2022 by Steve Jenkins
All rights reserved. No part of this book may be used or reproduced in any manner whatsoever without written permission except in the case of brief quotations embodied in critical articles and reviews. For information address HarperCollins Children's Books, a division of HarperCollins Publishers, 195 Broadway, New York, NY 10007.
clarionbooks.com

ISBN: 978-0-358-47011-3 hardcover
ISBN: 978-0-358-47014-4 paperback

The illustrations are cut- and torn-paper collage.
The infographics are cut-paper silhouettes and the graphics are created digitally.
The text type was set in Proxima Nova.
The display type was set in Berthold Akzidenz Grotesk.

Manufactured in Italy
ROTO 10 9 8 7 6 5 4 3 2 1
4500846239

First Edition